IMAGES
of America

RED BANK
VOLUME II

Welcome to Volume II. The same sign greets visitors at key entrances, including Coopers Bridge, Front Street and Shrewsbury Avenue, and Shrewsbury Avenue and Newman Springs Road. *Red Bank Volume I* was Arcadia's largest seller in 1995, evidencing the fact that this is a town interested in its history as well as a vibrant place where commercial, cultural, and social stimulation is high. The content of this book is new, and it is independent of the earlier work. However, frequent reference is made to Volume I to aid comparison of sites and pictures. (Photograph by Bridget Patalano.)

2

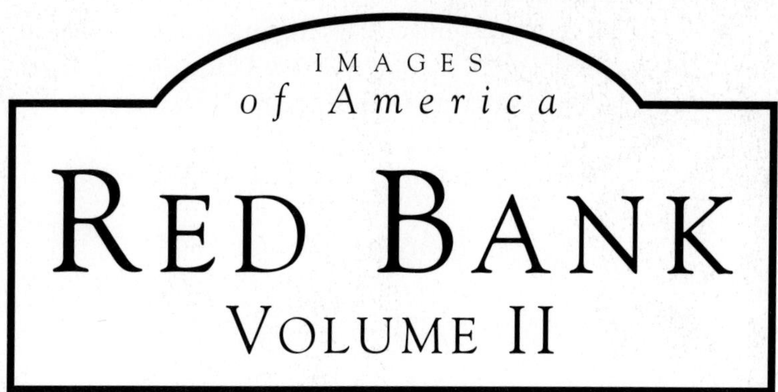

Randall Gabrielan

First published 1996
Copyright © Randall Gabrielan, 1996

ISBN 0-7524-0402-4

Published by Arcadia Publishing,
an imprint of the Chalford Publishing Corporation
One Washington Center, Dover, New Hampshire 03820
Printed in Great Britain

Library of Congress Cataloging-in-Publication Data applied for

Dearest Barbara Ann,
For all you do, this book is for you.
—Love, your husband, the author

Contents

Acknowledgments

Assembling the list of picture contributors is one of the most pleasant parts of these projects. Forty-four lenders reflect a broad, community-wide support that the author cherishes and for which he is most grateful.

Photography Unlimited by Dorn's is widely recognized as an unequaled source for local vintage photographs, although only part of their holdings have heretofore been available. Between volumes, the author has been working with Kathy Dorn Severini to identify, qualify, and help make available unprocessed negatives. Some of the first views in their newly-expanded collection are shown here.

Bernard Kellenyi, architect of some of the region's most significant buildings, has enjoyed a near fifty-year practice in Red Bank, a span permitting his early work to be viewed in a historical context. My thanks for the fine collection of 1950s views and renderings that helped the author attain a goal to lengthen this book's look at Broad Street.

Scott Longfield has long and skillfully photographed the author's writings for *The Two Rivers Times*, taking an informed and collaborative approach. It is a pleasure to publish two of Longfield's photographs in this work, although they are admittedly examples chosen for historical interest rather than as exemplars of his fine photographic talents.

A special word of thanks to three collectors who have given the author liberal access to their fine holdings: John Rhody, Robert Schoeffling, and Michael Steinhorn.

My thanks to all lenders, the true co-producers of this work, including: Elizabeth "Betsy" Albert, Jane Bartlett, Olga Boeckel, Francis and Margaret Borden, Ruth J. Breuer, Michael Cassone, Donald Dewey, Richard F. Doughty, Joseph Eid, Alexander J. Finch, First Baptist Church of Red Bank, Alma Harrison, Les Horner, Catherine Ann Jacoby, Margaret "Peg" Jordan, Jack Kaney, David Kennedy, Michael J. Kennedy Jr., Patricia Keiper Kurdyla, Evelyn Leavens, John Lentz, the Monmouth County Historical Association, George Moss, Daniel, Mary, and Bridget Patalano, the Red Bank Woman's Club, Alice Robinson, Anna Louise Campbell Rudner, Antoinette "Dolly" Salvatoriello, Karen L. And Leon Schnitzspahn, David and Karen Swenson Todd, Keith Wells, Lawrence E. White, and Marilyn Willis.

My special appreciation goes to those who took the initiative to seek out the author with their offers of help. I hope their work, memories, and families have been suitably recorded for posterity.

Thanks to Timothy J. McMahon of Fair Haven for sharing his memories of Red Bank.

Introduction

The writing of the second *Red Bank* volume in as many years accomplished some goals unmet by the first. This book gives a longer look at Broad Street's evolution, a more thorough examination of the railroad, and offers a better representation of the West Side.

A changing Broad Street is a microcosm of Red Bank history. The street grew in less than two generations after the 1870s from a short business street with a modest collection of houses to an attractive, thriving commercial center with a fine residential stem home to wealthy and influential citizens. As recently as the 1950s, one could attend to nearly all of life's needs on Broad Street. This book takes an expansive look at Broad Street in the 1950s, with special emphasis on storefront designs of the period. The classic image may be a horse and trolley-filled Broad Street, but store changes in the last forty years have been as extensive as in the forty years prior to 1956.

Changes on Broad Street are ongoing, as evidenced by a retail mix that increases steadily its vendors of fashionable material objects and life's smaller luxuries. Perhaps two decades into the next century a historian may analyze whether this process was a minor trend of the late twentieth century, or the path to sustained vigor for small-town main streets.

Maritime traffic provided the lifeline for this riverfront town from the early nineteenth century. The coming of the railroad in 1861 produced a building boom and housing storage. The railroad opened a transportation link to the south and created an opportunity to avoid the difficult Navesink River segment on transit to New York, once problematic bayshore connections were overcome. An enhanced presence of the railroad in this volume reinforces its significance in Red Bank.

The term "West Side" was first coined c. 1900 by Theodore White, an astute real estate developer who envisioned Red Bank's growth in that direction. The small lot division of the West Side influenced affairs beyond its borders, as parts of then Shrewsbury Township south of Newman Springs Road were similarly sub-divided. The Borough of Shewsbury was formed, in large part, to preclude similar development.

The West Side early became home to two groups of newcomers, Italian immigrants and later, African-Americans. The author was successful in obtaining fine pictures of the Italian population, but African-Americans are under-represented herein. This condition reflects the key challenge to an Arcadia author: obtaining rare images of known worthy subjects.

Chapter headings are retained for Front Street, a thoroughfare as interesting as Broad, and the waterfront, a subject with rich pictorial resources.

The author approaches local history as a continuous chain linked with the present. Although recent events and changes can be preserved through photography, we may not be able to understand their historical significance until much later, when we place them in context. The 1959 opening of the Monmouth Shopping Center, as Monmouth Mall was earlier called, is one of the most important events in Red Bank history. Its effect, the transformation of Broad Street, has been documented pictorially. Another external change impacting Red Bank is the suburban development of the surrounding towns.

Many of Red Bank's large houses, the former homes of its business and professional leaders, have been demolished or adapted for non-residential use. The houses along the north side of Riverside Avenue have been totally effaced. Red Bank's interest in its history and its rich pictorial archives will produce a third volume. One hopes its fine houses will be better represented. The author is accessible and seeks contact with those willing to lend pictures for copying for the next work. Contact him at (908) 671-2645, or write to 71 Fish Hawk Drive, Middletown, NJ 07748.

Errata: Volume I
Several points in *Red Bank Volume I* require correction at this time:

p.27 bottom
The picture depicts the east side of Broad Street.
p.100 bottom
The view is north.
p. 101 top
The caption did not make clear that the photograph is a composite of several Eisner locations.
p.103 bottom
The remark about the windows was gratuitous. They have been re-installed in the remodeled building.
p.118 top
Triangle Esso was at the juncture of Front, Riverside, and Pearl, the site of the Triangle Park.
p.123
The location at bottom was incorrectly identified. The Pleasant Inn (top) was a successor of an expanded Mecca Inn, the building located on the northwest corner of Newman Springs Road and Shrewsbury Avenue.

One
Broad Street

The procession of buses north on Broad Street is believed to mark the day when trolley service ended. The Boro Bus Company provided replacement surface transportation.

This early 1890s cyanotype by Edward Taylor, a noted photographer of Middletown, captures the essence of attempting to traverse Broad Street during unpleasant weather conditions. The block south of Front Street that would remain intact for decades is largely built, excepting the northeast corner with Mechanic Street where the Saltz Building would be constructed in 1903. (Collection of the Monmouth County Historical Association.)

Spinning & Patterson,
Dealers in
GROCERIES.
DRY GOODS, NOTIONS,
Hosiery. White Goods, etc.
Mm. Demorest's Reliable Patterns.

Cor. Broad and Front Streets,
RED BANK, N. J.

FOREST FLOWER COLOGNE,

The Richest and most Fashionable
Perfume Known.

Its Permanence and Delicacy of Odor have won for it the

FRONT RANK.

Accept no Other. SEE OUR NAME BLOWN IN BOTTLE.

For sale by all Druggists and Fancy Goods Dealers.

Price 25 cents, 50 cents and $1.00 per Bottle.

Trial Size 15 Cents per Bottle.

MANUFACTURED BY

W. J. AUSTEN & CO., - - OSWEGO, N.Y.

NEW YORK OFFICE, | CHICAGO OFFICE,
106 Duane St. | 154 Lake St.

The nature of nineteenth-century retailing can be inferred from the diverse product lines of Spinning & Patterson. Benjamin Spinning bought an early frame store on the southwest corner of Broad and Front (Volume I, p. 9), erecting the building pictured on the top of p. 11. This trade card from the Moss Archives dates to c. 1870s.

Jacob Kridel arrived in New York from Austria in 1871 with his brother. After the two traveled across the country, holding short-term jobs and engaging in itinerant sales, Jacob opened a dry goods store in Red Bank in the mid 1890s. Success followed. Kridel bought the Spinning & Patterson building *c.* 1913 and remodeled it, installing large display windows. The front was rebuilt again in the late 1940s, this view probably reflecting that change. What is the reader's favorite memory of Dugan's Bakery, at left? How about the cupcakes with hard icing, which, as the years pass, seems to have been a half-inch thick? (The Dorn's Collection.)

Demorest's Monthly Magazine was a leading periodical presenting Madame Demorest's "Mirror of Fashions" in conjunction with fiction, verse, and music. The publication was amply illustrated with patterns and prints of the latest styles. Spinning & Patterson advertised the availability of Demorest's patterns there. This illustration is from the April 1869 issue.

The crowd is too small for a parade. Is the cavalry troop drilling or on the move? This photograph of an event on the northernmost stem of the west side of Broad Street was obviously taken during the World War I era. One looks at the eight-bay Child Building for a clue as to the date, but the front does not provide evidence of whether the scene occurred before or after their March 3, 1917, fire. The Hance Building looks as if it could use the remodeling the Broad Street National Bank would give it a few years later.

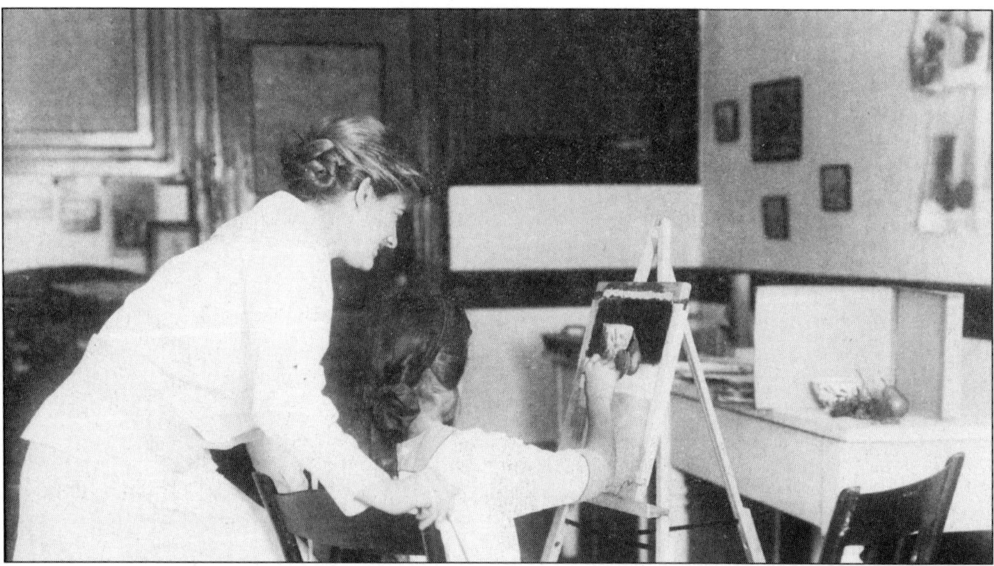

Georgie Burton Hazard, a native of Rhode Island, married Bowdoin Hazard, son of the Shrewsbury ketchup manufacturer and New York wholesale grocer Edward Clarke Hazard, in 1906. She advertised art classes at the Broad Street Studio of photographer Joseph Dickopf by 1914, noting that she was a pupil of the well-known Theodore Spicer Simeon of Paris. Georgie had an office in the Broad Street Child Building by 1920, the likely site of this photograph dating from around then. See p. 60 for the school she founded at Front Street.

Red Bank Methodism traces its origins back to the 1780s when services were said by circuit preachers. Later meeting at the Forum (p. 121) and jointly with Rumson Methodists, Red Bank Methodists bought a lot on the west side of Broad Street opposite Mechanic Street and built the First Methodist church there in 1845-6. It was rebuilt in 1867, as depicted in this image. This church was destroyed in the November 5, 1882, Child's Bakery fire that burned most of the block. When it became enveloped by the business district, the church decided to move to the still residential area located little more than a block to the south (p. 30).

The spire of the First Methodist Church stands tall on the west side of Broad Street as much of the east side smolders during the New Year's Eve fire that began in Jacob Naftal's menswear store. (See Volume I, p. 11.) This is a photograph of a drawing made for a newspaper from a photograph of the site. Newspapers of the time did not yet have the capability to print photographs.

The large space carved out for parking cars may be the most immediately impressive feature of this 1960s view. Broad Street is at the bottom, Monmouth Street is at left, and Front Street with the Navesink River is at right. White, the "great parking street," is inside their circle. Broad Street is largely intact, excepting the mid-block buildings south of Front which were destroyed by fire in 1978 (see p. 22). The former Sears building (p. 112) can be seen on White, a block west of Broad, while the Eisner Building (p. 29) stands out between White and

Monmouth. Front Street was then intact, not only including the Riverside Gardens Apartments, but also the store east of Boat Club Court, at right, destroyed by fire in the early 1970s. This view pre-dates "The Bluffs." The old Central Hotel on the Opera block, demolished in 1995, can be seen where Front and Riverside Avenue form a V at the fold. The picture post-dates the removal of the Triangle service station, also at the V.

Broad Street is decorated for the summer carnival. A large crowd gathers to view one of its most popular events, the decorated automobile parade.

A World War I-era parade, perhaps a post-war celebration, has brought out a large crowd to view the southward marching men. The area in the background by the trees was still residential.

A children's parade of the mid-to-late 1920s appears to take only half the street. The signage indicates change: "Weis'" has been removed from the Temple of Fashion sign and Reussille's has attached a placard to its building. (The Dorn's Collection.)

The snow scene on northern Broad Street appears to have been taken in the early 1920s. One suspects the bread delivery man has just left Child's. The view effectively shows storefronts on the east side of Broad, which are so often obscured by awnings. (The Dorn's Collection.)

Jersey Central Traction Company car no. 30 is followed by a Monmouth Electric Company series 20 car as both travel south, or clockwise as this direction of the circuit was known, on Broad Street *c.* 1910. H.N. Supp's store is the present Clayton and Magee.

Ludlow Hall, known today as Clayton and Magee's building, rented an upper floor to the Grand Army of the Republic Post No. 61. The group's meeting area is shown with the post's memorabilia *c.* 1910.

Remodeling Tetley's 17 Broad Street front in the walking town of Red Bank was an early project for architect Bernard Kellenyi. The store was designed to make maximum use of artificial light. The awnings were newly recessed, while Carrara glass was a popular decorative finish, with the recessed doors increasing window display space. A re-designed front for a clothing store now has minimal display space; a simple door is flush with the building line. The Tetley news and stationery business was begun in Red Bank *c.* 1883 by Civil War veteran John T. Tetley.

Bernard Kellenyi's 1955 storefront for Beverly Anderson's music store at 21 Broad Street differs in concept from his earlier work at Tetley's. Carrara glass is still used, but the storefront is designed to direct the viewer's eye inside the store, not merely to display merchandise. Later change has removed this image.

The west side of Broad south of Front in the 1940s was the site of many familiar buildings with their old, now unfamiliar fronts. What is one difference between the old and new Red Bank? On this street, one could buy footwear in three shoe stores located only a few doors apart from one another. Soon one may be able to buy a café latte at three nearby coffee shops—er—make that shoppes.

The Broad Street National Bank bought the Robert Hance & Sons store at 12 Broad Street in 1921. It is the building at left and also on the top of p. 12, looking nothing like a prospective banking headquarters. The bank made extensive alterations designed by Perth Amboy architect J. Noble Pierson, changing the overall appearance of the building. Companion before and after images may be found in Volume I on the bottom of p. 12. The bank's large vault weighed a reported 200 tons. The first floor was remodeled for stores, with new changes ongoing as the book is completed in August 1996. (The Dorn's Collection.)

H.E. Schroeder established a pharmacy at 16 Broad Street in 1870. The business retained his name while passing through several changes in ownership. By the early years of this century, it claimed to be the oldest in Monmouth County. The picture is undated, but likely post-dates the fire of 1882 which destroyed most of the block. (Collection of the Monmouth County Historical Association.)

The Merchants Trust Company building was erected in 1927 on the site of the former First National Bank building at 30 Broad Street. It can be discerned on the bottom of p. 23 as the first lower structure after the row of three-story buildings. The place was designed by Hoggson Brothers of New York, bank specialists who were both architects and general contractors. The Broad Street facade is granite, with brick cladding on the three other sides. The building was remodeled into retail space and sits vacant in August 1996 with this year's closing of longtime occupant, Carrolls Stationers. (The Dorn's Collection.)

This late 1940s view of the west side of Broad looking north shows an intact row of brick Commercial Italianate buildings, their signage exhibiting restraint. (The Dorn's Collection.)

A fire in November 1978 destroyed nos. 28 and 26 Broad Street. This picture was inserted not only to record a rare instance of the total replacement of buildings in the business district, but to portray how signage inappropriate to a historic area can mar the streetscape. The replacement building, numbered 26, was of dark brick with a round arch design motif. It blends well with Broad's predominant architectural style.

M.M. Davidson had occupied part of the Chadwick building on the west side of Broad Street for twenty-six years before buying it in 1909. Architect Joseph Swannell designed a remodeled store to make the entire building Davidson's clothing store, which formally re-opened in November 1910. Davidson was an innovative retailer, selling discounted merchandise by mail order and with promotional sales long prior to the era when nearly all clothes were sold off-price. (Collection of Michael Steinhorn.)

This c. 1907 postcard shows the west side of Broad Street. The Reussille store is at left, with its neighbor on the north containing Davidson's (prior to his 1910 remodeling into one store). Note the trolley switch track in the foreground.

Jack Kaney, a twelve-year-old student at St. James School in 1936, discovered one lunch hour how to reach the Eisner Building roof at 54 Broad Street. Taking his Rodenstock folding camera the next afternoon, he stealthily returned and took this picture. The lens must have had a long focal length, as the viewer appears suspended over the White Street intersection. The Register building and the Broad Street National Bank are the two taller structures at left, while the Wild Building on the corner and the Temple of Fashion with the cornice medallion are two recognizable landmarks at right.

The precise date of this early 1940s fire has escaped the collective memory of Prown's, the current trade name of National. (National is still Prown's corporate name.) The store was on the east side of Broad Street. This fire appears to have been minor; a serious blaze in the 1960s perhaps erased recollection of the earlier one and occasioned the store's February 1961 move to the west side, into the former Davidson building pictured on the top of p. 23. Note the cumbersome photography rig.

Charles Straus, assisted by his father Morris, bought the George W. Hance dry goods business in 1896, expanding his Broad Street store in 1908. He expanded again in 1912, constructing a major one-story building on the north in place of the shops pictured above. The store's 52-foot frontage was then one of the largest in Red Bank. Their large expanse of windows gave them the nickname, "the daylight store." (The Dorn's Collection.)

Straus had expanded to the place on the left prior to Bernard Kellenyi's 1955 project to unify the separate sections of the two fading, older stores. More of the wall between them was removed and the facades were joined by uniform cladding. Kellenyi designed the S in this manner to help link the one-and two-story buildings. Straus went out of business in 1966. A 1996 remodeling of now separately tenanted stores emphasizes their separation.

A crowd is gathered in front of the Register building, perhaps in the early 1950s, likely awaiting the arrival of the paper. The two young boys are probably street vendors. No one is waiting for "the number," however, as the *Register* was still a weekly. (The Dorn's Collection.)

W. Harry Pennington began a fifty-five-year career with the *Red Bank Register* as a printer's apprentice at age fourteen. Seven years later he was placed in charge of the composing room and made a junior partner. Pennington became president and one of three principal stockholders in 1959. Seen here in a 1930s photograph from the *Monmouth Pictorial*, he worked beside his men well after attaining an executive role. Pennington served in World War I, was a member of the Monmouth Boat Club and the Red Bank Elks, and was a justice of the peace. He died in 1968, earning a partner's tribute as "one of the finest, kindest men [he] ever knew."

26

The *Register* in the 1930s billed itself as the "Home Newspaper." Note that the corner store was two stories high and the White Street parking was free. The *Register* moved to this longtime home in 1897, after renting at the corner of Front (see Volume I, p. 10) and in the Hendrickson & Applegate building. (*Monmouth Pictorial*, Autumn/Winter 1936.)

An unidentified parade, *c.* early 1960s, pauses at the corner of Broad and White Streets. Fanny Farmer ended its long-term tenancy in 1996. The structure was the subject of a zoning controversy as defined by building inspector Ensley White in 1939. When the building was reduced to one story, White maintained that the planned alterations amounted to the new construction of a frame building, which was no longer permitted in that zone. A glance at the 1996 remodeling revealed very little of any structural element above the foundation. The building has a Broad Street frontage of only 16 feet, 8 inches, but extends 94 feet on White Street.

The William Haddon house, at right, once occupying the southwest corner with White Street, was moved *c.* 1880s to permit construction of the stores still on the site. The corner store must have had a monopoly, as it advertises its products but not its name. A morning crowd waits outside Phil Stoffel's tobacco store, perhaps for a smoke, or for the card game on the cover of Volume I. The street was long known as the Haddon block. (The Dorn's Collection.)

Phil Stoffel's Broad Street tobacco store is depicted here. The subject is not identified, and one wonders if he is Phil. The back of the store was the site of the card game on the cover of Volume I. Perhaps this fellow could not join, as his blurred image indicates a tendency to flinch. Everything in the store *c.* 1920 would be a desirable collectable today. How about the "Segar" sign? (The Dorn's Collection.)

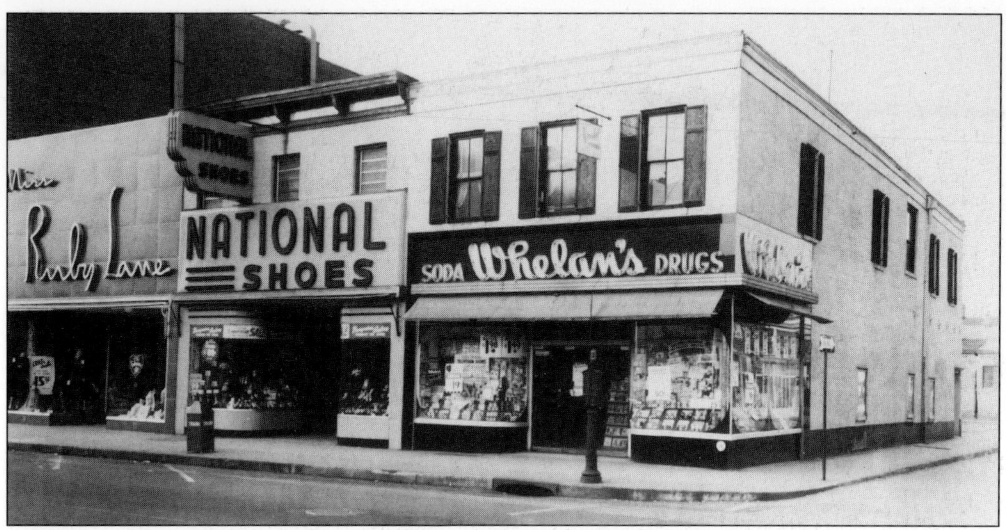

Whelan's made real estate news in 1922 by taking a twenty-one-year net lease on the corner and also buying the James Cooper pharmacy opposite it. It took a while to move into the occupied store; a glimpse of an early Whelan's front appears on the top of p. 27. By the time of this 1950s photograph, the building was extended on the west and the fronts had changed. The corner is now the longtime home of The Royal Box, Red Bank's most appealing gift store. (The Dorn's Collection.)

The Eisner Building, completed in early 1911 at 54 Broad Street, was built on the site of John Sutton's home and designed by Leon Cubberley of Long Branch. The George Hance Patterson stores are to the left, completed in 1905 (see Volume I, p. 54). The basic appearance of the building remains similar to that depicted in this c. 1912 postcard. Woolworth's is still a tenant, with the Red Bank location thought to be the chain's oldest continuously operating store. First-floor space was later altered to house a single store, with the office entrance relocated to the south. An Eisner organization still owns the building, maintaining an office there.

Red Bank Methodists bought the lot on the southwest corner of Broad and Monmouth Streets in December 1882, the month after fire destroyed the edifice pictured on p. 13. Its residential character was only suggested three decades later in this *c.* 1913 postcard, with Monmouth Street on the right. This Gothic Revival church was dedicated on March 2, 1884. Grace Methodist, a second church of that denomination, was little more than a block away (Volume I, p. 36) and the business district had reached Monmouth Street.

The First Methodist Church congregation had long talked about selling its Broad and Monmouth Street property and merging with the Grace Methodist Church. It was finally sold in 1940 to Newark real estate developers, who planned a store. The church had deteriorated, becoming a safety hazard at the end. This demolition scene is dated February 21, 1941. The Red Bank Mall is now on the site. (Collection of the Monmouth County Historical Association.)

This early 1950s image shows the west side of Broad Street looking south from the George Hance Patterson stores (right and Volume I, p. 24), now known as the Rocar Building. The three-story building on the corner of Monmouth is the Knickerbocker Building, built by Arthur Swift in 1910 (Volume I, p. 29). The one-story stores housing Liggett-Rexall Drugs and Schulte-United, built on the site of the First Methodist Church (p. 29), are on the southwest corner, with the tower of St. James in the background. (The Dorn's Collection.)

This image shows the same block that is depicted above, looking north in a dramatic 1980s view with Christmas lights. The Eisner Building (p. 29) is behind the traffic light.

This 1919 view of Broad Street looking south, likely taken from the Broad Street National Bank Building (p. 20) prior to its remodeling, shows the east side commercial buildings with points of three church spires in the background (the Grace Methodist Church is on the left, St. James is over the flagpole in the center, and the First Methodist Church is to its right). The new Red Bank Trust Company on the northeast corner of Wallace virtually glistens, its bulk nearly obscuring the Mercantile/Second National building on the southeast comer. The Wild Building is in the left foreground, while the Temple of Fashion is the two-story building with the cornice medallion. Can you spot Reussille's clock?

The c. 1950s interior of the Red Bank Trust Company bank at the northeast corner with Wallace reflects the building's original design by architect Warrington G. Lawrence. The view in recent memory was the redesign, perhaps dating from the 1960s, with a dropped ceiling and opened tellers' "cages." Banking ceased here in 1995. First Fidelity, which found itself with two Broad Street locations as a result of a merger, opted to retain its modern upper Broad Street bank, the one with the parking lot. (The Dorn's Collection.)

This *c.* 1910 view surveys the east side of the Broad block from one building north of Wallace Street. The street had been residential; one dwelling remains—the old Truex house between the coffee and express signs. Mrs. E. Weis began her millinery business in a rented store on Front Street. After two stores were destroyed by fire, she built the Temple of Fashion in 1895, the block's most distinctive building. The Wild Building at the north end can be seen in Volume 1 on p. 17. (Collection of John Rhody.)

The storefront at 53 Broad Street for Parke Drugs designed by Bernard Kellenyi as a "look-through," with the aim of directing the viewer's eyes to the merchandise inside, was the first in Red Bank to use Zourite, a striping of enameled aluminum panels. A later remodeling created a new front with more metal, less glass, and the elimination of the "look-through" effect, creating a look that is perhaps more suitable for the current optometrist occupant.

A parade is turning west from Broad on to Monmouth Street, likely in the 1920s, its exact time eluding the author even in the presence of numerous dating hints. Note the gas pumps in front of Fred H. Van Dorn's auto showroom. Van Dorn was reported to have tried a business then new to Red Bank when he opened the showroom in 1919, the parking of cars for a fee. Note the store, probably Alexander Chamber's pharmacy, built in front of the Borden house on the southeast corner of Linden Place, which extends past that block's established set-back building line. (The Dorn's Collection.)

Supermarkets dotted the townscape for about two decades after their late 1930s origin. However, they became unable to serve a clientele that became increasingly motorized. Acme, shown in the Whitfield Building (opposite Monmouth Street) in the early 1950s, chose a location north of Reckless Place several years later, but eventually moved to a strip center in Shrewsbury. (The Dorn's Collection.)

Scott Longfield recorded pictorially the 1992 transformation of the Strand Theatre for its present incarnation as offices. The 1927 murals painted for the reopening of the 1917 Strand were still in place when the building was remodeled.

A March 2, 1927, *Register* account of the reopening of the Strand claimed that the large number of life-size mural paintings were created by one of the foremost experts in the field, but it did not mention the artist's name. The murals were defaced during remodeling, typically in critical parts of the compositions, with this example not as bad as some others.

Architect Joseph Swannell's early plans for the Romanesque Revival St. James Catholic Church, completed in 1894 on the west side of Broad Street, indicated a full tower. One was not built, as evidenced by early photographs, including one in Volume I on p. 34. The Swannell-designed tower, added in 1911, is 90 feet high and was built of white stone with limestone trim by Alfred Mayo. This view from the Dorn's Collection was taken around the time of the tower's completion. The color difference is stark. Although time has blended new and older parts, the distinction is still visible.

His Excellency John C. Reiss holds the distinction of being the first native from the Trenton Diocese to rise to its head. He was born on May 13, 1922, in Red Bank, one of eleven children. Reiss was ordained a priest on May 31, 1947, and consecrated a bishop on December 12, 1967. Holding a number of official and parish positions after his consecration as he had previously, Reiss was installed as the eighth bishop of Trenton on April 22, 1980, an office he still holds as he plans retirement in 1997. His motto on installation will serve all well, always: "Let us love one another."

St. James chancel has changed since this *c.* 1920s view. The altar was built in 1916 of Carrara marble as a memorial to the Reverend James A. Reynolds. It remains in place with the front—a carving of the Last Supper—remounted on a part of the altar separated for contemporary worship practice. The raised pulpit has been replaced with one standing on the floor. The walls were artfully repainted and the rail removed.

The E.J. Reilly moving van was photographed on Broad Street around 1920. (The Dorn's Collection.)

Henry L. Zobel bought the property at the southeast corner of Broad and Harding Road in 1925 and demolished the Grace Methodist Church on the site in 1928. He then built this Italian Renaissance revival automobile showroom and office, designed by Vincent C. Eck, a Red Bank architect. Eck's practice was primarily ecclesiastical for the Catholic church. This 1950s view was made during the long-term tenancy of auto parts dealer J. H. Kelly Co. The lower flood was remodeled *c.* 1980 as offices, with the building hardly recognizable today. (The Dorn's Collection.)

Charles Lewis built the stores and offices with a 96-foot frontage north of the Strand Theatre in 1928 on the site of Van Dorn's garage. They were initially occupied as the J. Schwartz furniture and household goods store. Newberry's occupied this store only by 1940, their success by this *c.* 1950 picture resulting in expansion to the Whitfield Building. Tenants have changed often, even once including a McDonald's (see Volume 1, p. 27). The part of the block from the Whitfield Building north to Wallace Street is intact, but the Strand remodeling, which embraced the Lewis Building, changed the southern segment beyond recognition. (The Dorn's Collection.)

The scene of knee-deep water during the Saturday, July 29, 1961, street flooding was the most remarked-about photograph in Volume I. Was this woman's anguished call over the obviously wet interior of the car, or were her own needs greater than the vehicle's? Note the former residential set-back line at the southwest comer of Broad and Peters Place.

The speed of the 5.5 inches of rain overwhelmed the drainage system. The west side of Broad appeared to be in better condition. However, neither the time span between the two photographs nor the continued effectiveness of the brooms is known.

Acme had been located in the Whitfield Building (p. 34), so the spot near Leroy Place may have appeared "out in the country" by comparison. The 1950s pylon was built to attract the motorist's eye. However, the town's congestion moved south, increasing traffic flow and parking woes around supermarkets. This building, shown in a rendering from architect Bernard Kellenyi's office, is now the bank and office at 170 Broad Street, its surface covered in stucco.

The Holy Name Society's 1949 parade is viewed at the northeast corner of Broad and Harding Road, a spot that would be home to stores soon after. The Dr. William Matthews house is at left.

H. Raymond Eisner built this house on the east side of Broad Street in 1913. It was an Italian Renaissance Revival designed by Ernest Arend; the style was one of the architect's favorites and the house was not unlike his own house on Broad's northeast corner with Bergen Place (Volume I, p. 39). H. Raymond was a son of Sigmund and became president of the Sigmund Eisner Company. The grounds were expanded by three acres in 1916 which permitted a larger garden. The site is now a bank. (*Asbury Park Press*, October 10, 1916, pictorial supplement.)

Gustave Schwartz's Colonial Revival near the southwest corner of Reckless Place, built c. 1900, was named One Acre, suggesting the size of the lot purchased from the Reckless Estate. The mature trees date from Anthony Reckless's residency to the south (p. 44). One wonders if the dog expected a handout from the photographer for his dignified pose. The corner was later site of the Presbyterian church. An office is on the site now.

This *c.* early 1940s view south from Broad and Wikoff Place, the corner pictured below, shows the 1931 Elks Building in the left foreground and Costello's gas station (opposite) behind it. The railroad in the distance is crossing the Red Bank border with Shrewsbury. (The Dorn's Collection.)

This *c.* 1940 view looking south from the Elks Club is directed at the northwest corner of Broad Street and Wikoff Place. The spot is occupied by the Charles K. Champlin house, built in 1925 after he retired from the stage. The house, architect unknown, is bungalow-style with a roof simulating thatch. The house, long an upper Broad Street landmark, retains its integrity with an office now entered on the south. (Collection of John Rhody.)

The Oilrite Corporation of Red Bank built this Tudor Revival gas station, its artistic style demanded by the owners of the Lakeside development on the former Beyer farm. The architect was D. Wentworth Wright of Maplewood, and the location was the southeast corner of Broad Street and Pinckney Road. It belonged to Frank Costello on October 8, 1944, when he was photographed with Victor Patalano and his son Joseph. Red Bank's most attractive gas station was demolished to build the auto showroom below.

Extensive use of glass was unprecedented when Bernard Kellenyi designed the Rassas Pontiac showroom at 395 Broad Street in the late 1940s. The sloping glass was designed to minimize glare, but it was not widely available and manufacturers were not familiar with its design needs. Kellenyi worked with one to develop its special needs, completed the project with confidence, but admittedly watched the site carefully during the first storm following completion. The basic design is still intact at Rassas and has been copied often. The job was so long ago that this rendering is from the architect's own hand.

This c. 1902 view of the 1862 Italianate Anthony Reckless house designed by J.P. Huber reflects the grandeur of the former estate section of upper Broad Street. The greenhouse and side porch are gone, while a Colonial Revival front porch was added. The building, in a fine state of preservation, was listed on the National Register of Historic Places in 1983 in the name of its present owner, the Red Bank Woman's Club. Recognition and appreciation of the structure's stature are motivating factors in the current direction of a re-invigorated Club. (Collection of the Red Bank Woman's Club.)

The northeast first-floor room of the Reckless house was long known as the library, even in the absence of shelves. The Red Bank Woman's Club, having curtailed operations as a residential facility in 1995, is sharpening its focus to meet the next century, addressing self-growth and the needs of women. The club, motivated by a desire to preserve its cherished home—a common thread uniting its efforts—is also seeking to enhance the appreciation of Red Bank's history. The library, now a reception area, will newly serve to exhibit their collection of house-related memorabilia. (Collection of the Red Bank Woman's Club.)

44

Two

Front Street

George W. Bennett, one of several stage operators on the River Road route to Oceanic, may be one member of this unidentified trio. The content of the men's jugs is not identified either, but may be inferred as they are outside J.J. Antonides's liquor store. It is one of a block of still-standing brick stores on the south side of Front Street west of Emanual Court, known as Dugans Alley when this *c.* 1880s picture was taken.

The Schwartz automobile showroom at 141 West Front Street was architect Bernard Kellenyi's first commercial building. This *c.* 1949 streetscape has changed little over the past half-century, excepting the removal of the gas pumps whose presence influenced the design. Maurice Schwartz wanted to sell gas at a time when it was no longer common for a new car dealer to do so. The building's industrial design finish was red, with white letters, the color chosen by Schwartz to increase visibility.

The Baird-Davison Company, long a major dealer of farm machinery and supplies, was located at 176 West Front Street in a building readily recognizable decades after the company ceased operations.

46

Miner Supply Company at the southeast corner of Front and Pearl Streets had a fine frame Commercial Italianate style building erected *c.* 1860s. It may be remembered for two signs, one offering Peachy Plumbing Paraphernalia, and the other, beside a thermometer, inviting one who did not like the temperature to wait, both post-dating this early 1950s view. Pearl Street traffic then flowed north. The building was demolished in 1993 and a new row of modern stores was built on the block east to Maple Avenue in 1996. (The Dorn's Collection.)

George W. Ogilvie opened a carriage business in 1903 after many years employment in the field. After two changes of style, the firm was named Ogilvie and Brown and located at 35-37 East Front Street when pictured in the *New Jersey Standard* souvenir illustrated edition of March 29, 1907. They were proud of their representation of Studebaker. Note the John W. Stout house in the distance (Volume I, p. 48).

Any old imposing building slated for demolition has immediate nostalgia value. The former Central Hotel on the Opera block at Front's southwest corner with Maple Avenue opened in 1882. It contained small apartments in its later years of occupancy. One tenant was reported to have kept all his possessions, even the inedibles, in the refrigerator, as protection against the tiny creatures that ruled the building. Andrew Lustbaum opened a Chrysler showroom in one of the stores in 1927. The building was leveled in 1995 and replaced by a retail strip that runs to the end of the block at Pearl Street in 1996.

Scott Longfield photographed the author's favorite Red Bank sign in August 1994 for his review of *Roadside New Jersey* for *The Two River Times*. As the author notes, "I have long-wanted to comply literally with the sign and straddle the two lanes, but, of course, they mean 'Form Two Lanes.' Traffic is difficult enough there and no one likes a wise guy, so I conform." Note the Opera block in the background, since demolished as noted above.

Red Bank's many parade photographs were often unlabeled. This one from the 1920s is useful for showing the tall Hendrickson and Applegate building and the Globe Hotel east of it on the south side of the Front streetscape.

Jacob Rue was proud of having a large, combination automobile and boat launch facility when he built this garage at 32 West Front Street in 1908. The still-standing building is shown in Volume I on p. 47 with his name. Rue announced in 1909 that the growth in his marine business required his full-time attention. He leased the automobile section to Melvin R. Van Keuren of Eatontown. (The Dorn's Collection.)

This is likely the aerial view taken in 1915 by Spofford and Hughes and sold by subscription. There are few major dating clues as nearly all of downtown Red Bank was built by the 1906 construction of the Frick Lyceum, the large building at lower left. The blessing of a winter scene—no trees in foliage—brought the bane of a snow scene, perhaps covering details and keeping automobiles away. The five-story Peters/Hance/Broad Street National Bank building (p. 20) is in the lower right corner. Front Street runs up and down the right page. The side-gabled building on the north side (left) of Front, below the middle of the right page, is at the

street's northeast corner with Wharf Avenue. West of Wharf are the carriage sheds. The hipped-roof house in the open lot above the sheds is the house to which the hospital in Red Bank moved, giving Riverview its start on the riverfront. Note the mansard-roofed Conover house on the north side of Front (Volume I, p. 52) and the bell-shape towered house several buildings below it (Volume I, p. 48). The area is now a Riverview parking lot. Somewhere in the photograph is 59 East Front Street, Georgie Hazard's Burton Academy (p. 60). This is the author's favorite picture in this book. (The Dorn's Collection.)

This 1919 snapshot, likely taken from the Hance Building at 12 Broad Street (soon to be the Broad Street National Bank Building), provides a glimpse of the infrequently-seen horse sheds behind Front Street (center of photograph) and the inland side of the waterfront, where a steamer, likely the *Albertina*, is docked at the foot of Wharf Avenue. The side-gabled house, partially visible at right, had stores built into it by then. It was known as John's busy corner for John Bailey, who owned John's Bargain Store there and who bought the building in 1921. A farmers' market existed along Wharf Avenue. A bowling alley was in the three-story building at the left rear. The storefronts along Front change periodically, but the block is largely intact.

Research by Bob Ebner, owner of the Front Street "hole-in-the-wall" at the foot of Broad, indicates that this passage has existed as a right-of-way for property owners on the west since at least 1850. Motorists formerly could drive through, a feat that the author needed to endeavor only once to realize driving there should be barred as a safety hazard, which it was in 1983. The antique pole outside Domenick's Barber Shop, where the author gets trimmed what little hair he has remaining, is gone, having succumbed to both four-wheeled and two-legged predators. A small replacement hangs on the side of the building.

The Globe Hotel on the south side of Front Street east of Broad was such a center of activity that one imagines Charles Foxwell had to rise early to photograph it in morning solitude. Its origin was a home built *c.* 1840 by Robert Hart; its end was a fire on December 19, 1936. It was enlarged several times in between.

Henry Carroll's saloon is believed to have been located in an unidentified building on West Front Street. It is a handsome structure, considering that aesthetics were not an important criterion for a watering hole. However, the brackets, nice cornices, and good balance give this mid-nineteenth century building a touch of class. The girls probably did not. Henry is the man in the center. The occupation of the rough-looking character on the right is unlisted, but as with the second-story belles, can likely be inferred. (The Dorn's Collection.)

The 1893 George R. Lamb Building (Volume I, p. 49), built as a liquor store, is the most prominent in the row of stores to its east, which has been intact for a century. The places beyond the Stout house (Volume I, p. 48) have now been sacrificed to a parking lot. DeSotos have sneaked into two of the author's books this year, but in this case the car is represented by a dealership. Globe's building was demolished in the 1960s and replaced with the high-rise medical office at 21 East Front Street. (The Dorn's Collection.)

After seven years of bicycle dealing in Asbury Park, W. Mahns opened a Red Bank sales and repair shop at 21 East Front Street in 1910. He represented Iver Johnson, Hudson, Dayton, and Pierce, but also claimed the place was a "mecca" for used bicycles. Mahns sold parts and did repairs here while his brother maintained the shop on the shore. One can presume this is he from the July 1911 number of *American Suburbs*.

Norman Deacy's service station was located at 111 East Front Street just west of the bridge below. Diminutive buildings on small lots made up much of the major expansion of the number of gasoline outlets in the 1930s. Note the exterior lift. A copy shop is now on the site. (*Monmouth Pictorial*, Autumn/Winter 1936.)

Throckmortons Gully once included a recognizable body of water. Throckmortons Bridge today spans a tiny stream, and marks the separation of Front Street and River Road, which is actually a continuous thoroughfare.

The Elks bought the Samuel T. Hendrickson house on the south side of East Front Street east of the Globe Hotel in 1913. The Italianate house was built *c.* 1870; this photograph was taken *c.* 1920. Samuel died intestate in 1892, the house descending to his brother, J. Holmes Hendrickson. The fourteen-room house was adapted for a lodge with meeting rooms and overnight accommodations for visiting Elks. A major addition was built on the rear. (The Dorn's Collection.)

The present appearance of the large Colonial Revival house at the southeast corner of River Road and Throckmorton Street was created in 1916 by owner Roger Farquhar's expansion, which included construction of the two porches and the addition of bay windows on the east side, not visible in this photograph. The house was likely built *c.* 1900.

The Holy Trinity Evangelical Lutheran Church was built *c.* 1938 at 150 River Road just east of Throckmortons Gully and was designed by New York architects Cherry and Matz. The firm specialized in churches and had recently designed a number of small Lutheran churches elsewhere. The Colonial Revival church looks today as it did in this early 1940s view. The wing at the rear was built to provide side and basement entrances and to contain a sacristy.

The owner of this Shingle style-Colonial Revival house at the southwest corner of River Road and Throckmorton Street appears to have achieved a photographic "three-for" by combining his house, car, and family in one picture. The *c.* 1895 house is now the parish hall of the Holy Trinity Evangelical Lutheran Church.

Joseph C. Fisher, born 1826, the son of Leonard, owner of extensive New York real estate, bought part of the Nathan Cook estate in 1864 and several properties thereafter. He is believed to be the man in the center of this *c.* 1892 photograph in front of the tree, his right arm on the chair of his wife Elizabeth. Their eldest daughter Florence married James L. Phelps. Using known names and ages but without specific identification, one infers Florence is standing over the chair at left, with James and the Phelps children at right. Delford, later known as a sportsman, appears to be the banjo player, while his brother Malcolm is likely at left.

The Fisher home was near the Navesink River with a 55 Fisher Place address after that street was cut through the family's developed property. Family history indicates Joseph built this place using part of an older house's foundation. Plans for a larger house, styled consistently for the times, were never used. Mabel's will provided liberal provisions for her heirs, whose interests were bought by her son Samuel Tilton, who lived there until his death in 1989.

Joseph Fisher died in 1893, not long after the picture opposite was taken. His widow Elizabeth is seated at center, while daughter Mabel, who would survive to age 102, is seated at right. She married Albert E. Tilton, right. Fred Fisher is standing over Mabel. He owned the place on the bottom of p. 66 and is the grandfather of Elizabeth Albert, who lent the four pictures on these two pages and several others. Delford is at left (see also p. 67). The younger Florence Phelps (her mother is standing over Samuel) shows off her doll in front. Others are Fishers, excepting the unidentified woman standing at left.

The Fisher boathouse on the Navesink River is shown here on August 17, 1894. The residence was in poor condition at the time of Samuel's death, was sold, demolished *c.* 1994, and replaced by a new house.

Georgie Hazard, shown here in a *c.* 1910 photograph, conducted the Burton Academy at 59 East Front Street for nearly forty years until she was disabled by a stroke *c.* 1965. Art, languages, and tutoring were highlighted on Georgie's 1920s billhead, although the first was a Saturday extra in the later years. She was divorced from Bowdoin Hazard in 1917 and did not marry again. Instruction at the academy was individualized, with progress geared to a student's capabilities and needs.

The school rooms were on the first floor at 59 East Front Street, while the private quarters were upstairs. Georgie lived in the entire house, the two sections indivisible. The two principal classrooms were separated by an open arch. Although organized by younger and older pupils, the open arrangement created an opportunity for each student to hear all instruction; thus, students were often familiar with new material as they progressed. The house was acquired by Riverview Hospital after Georgie's death in 1965 and demolished as part of their parking lot on the north side of Front Street.

Three
Waterfront

A mass of people skating, boating, or just watching characterizes a typical winter sporting scene on the Navesink *c.* 1910.

Red Bank north of Front Street and West of Maple Avenue is not thought of as a peninsula, but this *c.*1980 aerial by Jack Lentz indicates that it is. The view is east, and the three bridges are, from top to bottom: Coopers, the New York and Long Branch Railroad, and Hubbards. Several waterfront landmarks are readily recognizable, including the Molly Pitcher Hotel (the building with the cupola) left of the fold, adjacent to the large parking lot; the Navesink House, the tall building right of the fold; Riverview Medical Center, the large building after the bend on Front

Street; and the no-longer standing Riverside Gardens apartments, below Riverview. The Eisner Factory, or Galleria, (p. 83), is right of center above the railroad tracks. Monmouth Street is the diagonal light space second from the right. The former Hoffmire House (Volume I, p. 38), the six-dormer place at bottom, is the site of the Senior Center, nearing completion in the summer of 1996. The S.S. Thompson Building (p. 103) is the tall building above the railroad.

The summer carnival was a town-wide recreational celebration with a variety of activities on land and river. The event, popular from the early years of this century, waned around World War I. This is a Foxwell real-photo postcard, its 1909 postmark likely reflecting the event's date.

Jane Bartlett, born a Hendrickson in Middletown, was a skilled powerboat racer. She is seen c. 1950 at the regatta with her J17 Beep, a Class M hydroplane, when she finished second.

Swimming while wearing flotation devices must have been difficult, but these three men, perhaps part of the Fisher family, appear to have accomplished it in 1894.

Guy Lombardo's presence in Red Bank helped make a success of the town's National Sweepstakes Regatta. This is his boat *c.* 1940. The author hesitated placing it in the book, because Lombardo is best remembered by Jane Bartlett (left) for having swamped her husband Irving's boat!

A winter sporting scene often needs little precise identification to convey the spirit of the masses enjoying themselves. This photograph was taken *c.* 1910 on the Navesink.

Fred Fisher's snack stand, shown here in a *c.* 1915 photograph, was a convenient eatery for winter sport participants and viewers. It was adjacent to the Wharf Avenue landing.

Delford Fisher, shown here in a *c.* 1910 Foxwell photograph, was born on September 17, 1875, the youngest son of Joseph and Elizabeth Dennis Fisher. He was a well-known winter sportsman, once heading the North Shrewsbury Iceboat and Yacht Club. He was also a member of the Monmouth Boat Club and Trinity Episcopal Church. Fisher never married and lived in the old Fisher house (p. 58) when he died in 1969 at age ninety-three.

Del Fisher is leading in a speed skating contest, photographed *c.* 1920. He was a sometimes house painter and managed four Broad Street stores inherited from his uncle John Marvin Dennis, activities that would not interfere with his sporting pursuits and travel.

Delford Fisher, a well-known ice boater, recalled some years later the subjects in this well-known *c.* 1900 scene at the North Shrewsbury Ice Boat and Yacht Club. James B. Weaver, the club commodore for whom a trophy is named, is seated at left. The second man to Weaver's left is boat builder Charles B. Irwin. In the rear, wearing a derby and tie and sporting a mustache, is *Register* reporter George Longstreet. The bearded man at right in the rear is George Haviland, another boat builder. (The Dorn's Collection.)

This ice boating scene was captured *c.* 1930s

Jack and James Casey were not the first to fly in the area, but they took aviation to new heights, literally and figuratively. Jack was an owner of the Red Bank Airport, and pioneered aviation advertising by dropping circulars from an airplane in 1920. Jack's reaching an altitude of 11,000 feet made headlines in 1920. This is the brothers' plane seen on the ice on February 14, 1920.

Class A ice boats are the largest sailing today; the category is defined by sail area, which is typically 350 square feet. These boats have Marconi rigs and are steered from the stern. The division between main and jib sails is typically 300 and 50 square feet respectively. This image represents a 1977 scene on the Navesink.

Jacob Rue's automobile garage is in front of the taller, pitched-roof building in this early 1950s photograph and in Volume I on p. 47. Rue also built a marine operation, which was sold to Hans Wulff and later to Irwin's Yacht Works in 1951. The building in the foreground was destroyed by fire *c.* 1967 and replaced with a taller, steel building, which is in operation as Irwin's Yard No. 2, handling larger craft.

The *Sea Bird*'s sixty-year career began in 1866, distinguishing the 187-foot long vessel as the Navesink's longest running. This *c.* 1910 real-photo postcard published by Dickopf's Art Shop captures the ambiance of a busy wharf at docking time. (Collection of Michael Steinhorn.)

Lionel Barrymore is much better known today for his acting career than for his artistic output. Few know of his fondness for the graphic arts, but he did have gallery exhibitions in his lifetime. Barrymore visited New Jersey, and several of his etchings have shore themes. This one, titled *Old Red Bank*, has resulted in speculation over its scene. However, it is likely a conjectural sketch from memory, done long after any local visit and intended as an evocation of the riverfront atmosphere rather than as a depiction of a specific spot. Many Barrymore plates were lost after his printer retired in 1938. This image was taken from a greeting card example of the work.

Riverview Medical Center had its Union Street origins in a residence, a former boarding house known as the Champlin House, moving there from rented Broad Street quarters in 1929. Numerous additions were made, this major one *c.* 1950, and the house of their origin, shown in the front of this *c.* 1954 photograph, was eventually demolished.

This view shows the entrance to Coopers Bridge *c.* 1910 looking west towards Middletown. The Coopers owned much land on the Middletown side, including the two houses pictured in the background. The one on the right was remodeled into offices at 7 Conover Lane, while the one on the left was destroyed by fire. This is the second Coopers Bridge, built *c.* 1862 and rebuilt in 1894, which replaced a low, crude structure built *c.* 1835

A celebration lasting into the night marked the May 5, 1926, opening of the present Coopers Bridge. A parade beginning with automobiles carrying local and county officials was followed by the Red Bank Cavalry troop and soldiers from Fort Monmouth. Temporary decorative arches included multicolored lights, flags, and bunting. A banquet, fireworks, a band concert, and dancing on the bridge were nighttime activities. Hardly anyone thought the bridge would be crumbling seventy years later, with a replacement planned as this volume is published.

Four
Railroad

The commuters' revolt of February 8, 1978, was sparked by the failure of the 4:49 train out of New York to stop as scheduled at Middletown. Angry passengers blocked the path of the train at Red Bank until given transportation back to Middletown (which was provided by several police cars and a bus). After years of poor service, the unprecedented, spontaneous protest helped galvanize public support for an on-going campaign for improved conditions, its short-term inconvenience to the remaining passengers of this train and those behind it notwithstanding.

The station of the Delaware and Raritan Bay Railroad, the predecessor of the New Jersey Southern and later Southern Division of the Central Railroad, was located on Morford Place north of Front Street and is shown here c. 1915. The road was announced by its backers as a route to southern New Jersey, with perhaps land connections over Delaware Bay, but the company actually conceived a competitive line to the Camden and Amboy Railroad, which enjoyed a state-sanctioned monopoly on the New York to Philadelphia route. Thus, its impact on local development was merely coincidental. (The Dorn's Collection.)

The freight station of the New Jersey Southern was adjacent to the passenger station. Freight was carried after passenger service was disbanded; this station was demolished in 1947. Judge Theodore Labrecque, on learning of its impending destruction, suggested that Dorn's preserve the image. Their effort has been reproduced often, as it is the only known view of the station. Although much of its Red Bank track is gone, this single track line of the New Jersey Southern can be followed on its route south. (The Dorn's Collection.)

Edward Taylor captured a moment of a busy morning at the Red Bank New York and Long Branch station *c.* 1895. The line was opened in 1875 and the station built that year. One wonders if standing on the tracks made the train arrive sooner. (Collection of the Monmouth County Historical Association.)

The Red Bank station had become worn and showed it. Its decorative vergeboard had disappeared and some voices called for its replacement. The station was restored instead, with the building today looking more like the picture at top than this image from *c.* 1975. (Photograph by Leon Schnitzspahn.)

This view shows the southbound Pennsylvania Railroad derailment of Friday, March 19, 1909; the locomotive in this wreck is shown in Volume I on p. 97. The rear axle of the last car, at left, and the pony wheels of the engine were the only ones not to leave the track. The odd angle of the middle coach made it difficult to walk through. One trainman was injured. (Foxwell real-photo postcard.)

The Chestnut Street switching tower on the south side is seen here in the 1970s with the crossing of the New York and Long Branch tracks in the foreground, running to the east. The single-track Southern line is to the right of the tower, adjacent to yard and side tracks present at that point.

Canadian Pacific #1286 was in Red Bank on June 25, 1967, for a fan trip to Bridgeton, in southern New Jersey sand country. Les Whitfield, then chief dispatcher, planned the route in 1966. Two fans are of great interest: Emily Tilton, crossing the tracks, is followed by her daughter Lora. Both have numerous service credits at several area historic sites. They did not make the trip but they arrived in the book, unaware they had been photographed that day.

The American Freedom Train Foundation organized a museum on rails for a bicentennial tour of the United States. It was a twelve-car panorama of American history, starting with our colonial origins and including material as new to us as lunar rocks. Exhibits ranged from the historically significant, such as George Washington's hand-annotated copy of a draft of the Constitution, to the entertaining, such as memorabilia from the worlds of sports and the performing arts. Will Arcadia books be in a tercentenary successor? Will there be rails left in 2076? The train is seen on its September 2, 1976, arrival in Red Bank.

A southbound train waits at the Red Bank station and is viewed from the Monmouth Street crossing in this *c.* 1910 photograph. The gates, blocking both lanes of traffic in each direction, required manual operation. The absence of an automatic signal made the trip around the rear of the train perilous. (The Dorn's Collection.)

Walter A. French, left, was photographed with an unidentified railroad employee at the Red Bank station. French was long a major liquor dealer and bottler of a variety of beverages. In 1882, he built the three-story French building on Broad Street that is one building south of the corner of Front and is visible on the bottom of p. 17. We may not know the occasion of this picture at the station, but it provides a fine example of a well-stocked newsstand of the time, one that carried *Harper's Bazaar*, which printed its issue date—August 1910—large enough to date the photograph.

The GG-1, the all-time classic American electric locomotive, pulled many a Red Bank commuter into New York's Pennsylvania Station, but not from the Red Bank station. The New York and Long Branch line was electrified only to South Amboy. Trains from points south entering New York had to switch to an electric locomotive, typically one of the GG-1s, which were built from 1934 to 1947. The engine had fast acceleration and reportedly could attain speeds of 130 miles per hour. This image, taken October 28, 1983, at the Matawan station, was a fan trip, final run of the GG-1, newly painted in Pennsylvania Railroad's colors, Tuscan red with gold stripes.

A Central Railroad camelback locomotive, No. 758, takes on coal at the Red Bank yard in 1950.

Extensive replacement of equipment was undertaken in the early 1980s. This train at the Red Bank station in November 1982 is pulled by an F40PH locomotive, the typical diesel that continues to be used on most Bay Head to Newark non-electric tracks.

After decades of talk and months of preparing foundations for wire poles, electrification below South Amboy began in 1981. A ceremonial opening of the segment to Matawan was made on April 24, 1982; this image was taken in a revenue run on Monday, April 26th. Electrification was soon extended to Red Bank and south to Long Branch.

Five

West Side

The term West Side was coined by Theodore White *c.* 1900 as he was selling building lots in a boom part of town. Much of the property was outside the town limits, as Red Bank, when first organized as a town within Shrewsbury Township, had as a southern border a line that ran east-west across town at the area of Irving Street. This *c.* 1930 picture from the Dorn's Collection shows at bottom the Red Bank Pirates' stadium on the south side of Newman Springs Road. The long building at center right is the River Street School. The incinerator stack is visible at left, adjacent to a bend in the Swimming River, the southwesterly tributary of the Navesink River.

Looking towards Coopers Bridge in the 1940s, Bridge Avenue had three active gas stations at its juncture with Rector Place and Riverside Avenue. Only one is open in mid-1996. (The Dorn's Collection.)

Sal Vaiti opened his tavern and restaurant at 141 Shrewsbury Avenue in November 1933. Still a popular eating and drinking place sixty-three years later, its crowds turn into massive throngs at the restaurant's Old Timers Day anniversary celebration each November when prices are rolled back to the 1930s. This view is c. 1950; the once-wide windows have now been bricked-up to small openings. (The Dorn's Collection.)

The Sigmund Eisner Company incorporated in 1916 with $500,000 capital, its business booming with a United States government contract for 1.5 million military garments, 150,000 mattress covers, and 50,000 mosquito nets. A surge in the number of employees demanded new space. The firm had been acquiring Bridge Avenue property in anticipation of expansion. The last house and the James Clayton store were moved in early 1917 for the construction of the three-story building at left, seen in 1984 before its remodeling into the collection of shops known as the Galleria.

In the raincoat factory, equipment "tantamount to a vulcanizer" bakes the coats for the United States Army. Cementers are at work in this picture. Note the identification badge on the man in the foreground, similar to that shown on p. 85. This and the following three pictures are from the April 1942 *Clothing Trade Journal*, lent by Gerald Eisner.

A large force of government inspectors was present during the war to assure finished goods were in compliance with contract standards. This photograph drew attention to the modern lighting overhead which facilitated the employees' work.

The Eisner cafeteria-recreation building was at the southeast corner of Bridge Avenue and Front Street. One could eat a brown-bag lunch there in the World War II era and it has been reported the building was available for off-hours social events.

Men are at work in Cutting Room 8 laying up cloth on a modern, automatic, 60-inch cloth spreader, with a marker at left. Cloth cutting was one of the most skilled and crucial operations, with rapidity as well as accuracy needed to maintain smooth-running production. See Volume I, p.100 for a picture of the older section of the factory.

Shown here is Mary D'Onofrio's identification badge from the plant they called "Eisner's College" because of its size and out of respect. She recalls them as a favored employer with friendly, respectful management and as a facility with a year-round operation. The war enhanced employment opportunities for women, who then had the chance to work in higher-skilled, better-paid parts of garment manufacture as the military took the men. When Brooklynite Daniel Patalano saw this face, he decided he was not returning home. The couple's marriage curtailed Mary's tenure at Eisner's; they still live in Red Bank and kindly lent the badge.

Florence Bell was born in New York City, the only daughter of James Bell and Lida Pearce Bell, he an Irish-born fabric importer, and she the London-born daughter of Sir Charles Edward Pearce. Red Bank, a former summer home, became the family's year-round domicile after Florence's father's death in 1913. She married Alfred D. Ilch after graduation from the Convent of the Visitation at age sixteen, and had two sons and one daughter. Florence Bell Ilch had grown up with dogs and horses, beginning her show experience at Westminster with a St. Bernard pup given for her ninth birthday.

Florence B. Ilch received her start with collies by buying one for her young sons. That dog fared poorly in a show, and she decided better dogs were needed. She bought three costly bitches, two of them champions. Mrs. Ilch, needing a stud, startled the dog world by paying $1,000 for this dog, Starbat Strongheart, at age nine months, after a show loss. The skeptics were again startled as Starbat Strongheart built an outstanding exhibition record over the next three years.

Michael J. Kennedy, born 1892 in Ireland, emigrated to America as a teen. After World War I service, he had a number of kennel positions and was Starbat Strongheart's handler at the show prior to his purchase by Florence Ilch. He shared her confidence in the dog, and was hired by Mrs. Ilch. He became kennel manager and handled all operations including breeding, show handling, and preparing dogs for sale. His affinity for collies was reflected in his soft tone and gentle kindness to his dogs. His importance and esteem were reflected by Mrs. Ilch, who acknowledged, "He has no peer." (Photograph given by Michael J. Kennedy Jr.)

The home of Bellhaven Kennels, founded in 1919, was 74 Locust Avenue, a house still standing and perhaps best seen in the winter from the Middletown side of the western stem of the Navesink River. Bellhaven had about 125 collies at its peak and was responsible for making the collie a top-ranking show dog, with Bellhaven dominating the breed in the years between the wars. Its last show dog was exhibited in 1962. Bellhaven closed in 1966, due in large part to Michael Kennedy's retirement, with older dogs living out their lives there. Mrs. Ilch died in 1982.

The emotive power of this September 1920 photograph of the D'Onofrio family can be best appreciated when one realizes that it was taken to send to loved ones in Italy to show the group had arrived in America and was beginning a new life. Wearing their fine old-country garments only a month after arriving, the family was headed by Patsy (at right), a banker in Naples who would become a carpenter here. His wife, Teresa, is at left, and daughter Jennie is in between. Their son Joseph would own Red Bank Electric Company. Daughter Louise (at left) would marry a Vaiti, while their youngest girl, Mary (center) would marry Daniel Patalano, and lend this picture for publication.

The P. Acquiviva Italian Band poses proudly, probably near River Street, on Columbus Day in1925. To the right of the drum in the suit is Professor Acquiviva, trained at the music school at La Scala, Milan. The clarinetist in the first row, third from the right is Louis Rampino, Mary Patalano's brother-in-law. (Photograph by Stewart, Red Bank.)

By the summer of 1944, Professor Acquiviva's musicians have been renamed the Red Bank Concert Band. A number of the musicians have likely been with him the entire period, such as Louis Montana, the trumpeter to his left in each picture. The group won numerous awards, but disbanded after Acquiviva's death not long after this picture was taken.

A campaign to build an Italian Catholic church was organized in 1917. A lot was purchased at the southeast corner of Bridge and Chestnut Streets *c.* 1918, deeded to the bishop of the Trenton diocese in 1919, with construction beginning in late 1920. A large, jubilant crowd assembled for a cornerstone-laying ceremony on Sunday, November 28, 1920. The church was named in honor of St. Anthony. It opened for worship in January and was dedicated by Bishop Thomas J. Walsh on Monday, May 29, 1921.

The Reverend Nicholas Soriano was appointed first pastor of St. Anthony's. He was born in Sperrone, Avellino, educated in Italy, and ordained in Rome in 1907. He came to the United States in 1913 and first served in New York. In 1936 (the year of this photograph), Father Soriano oversaw a church remodeling, including the addition of two chapels. Improved seating and a new altar are two changes made since.

Owner Morris Siegel stands outside while his brother Michael is behind the door in June 1971 as Morris planned to close Benny's Grocery. It was founded in 1931 at 185 Shrewsbury Avenue by Morris's brother-in-law Bernard Beterman and looked little-changed over forty years. A fine array of Italian specialties enabled the Jewish merchants to succeed in this ethnic neighborhood. The building stands, stuccoed over, taking away the 1920s retail design look.

The Red Bank Electric Company, founded by Joseph D'Onofrio, moved from River Street to the corner of Oakland and Bridge Avenue c. 1950, with the photograph likely not dating long afterwards.

Albert L. McQueen, shown here with hands on his hips, opened this grocery store on the southwest corner of Shrewsbury and Locust Avenues *c.* 1885. He served as overseer of the poor and was a member of the United American Mechanics and the Union Hose Co. Ruth Breuer (née Clayton) is the child with her mother Jennie to her left and her grandmother Lydia McQueen to the right.

The McQueen store was well-stocked *c.* 1920s.

The Red Bank Reformed Church at Shrewsbury Avenue and Leonard Street appears in Volume I on p.108 in pre-remodeling condition. This c. 1940 view reflects the 1915 remodeling and expansion. The most visible changes are the removal of the tower and the rebuilding of the east facade. The building was sold to its present owner, the Pilgrim Baptist Church, in 1955; the Reformed congregation built a new edifice on Hance Road in Tinton Falls.

Jimmy Galatro and his nephew Willie ran the G & G Service Station at the southwest corner of Shrewsbury Avenue and Catherine Street. Jimmy held the water can while Willie had his hands in his pockets on November 6, 1937, when the two were photographed with a group of friends. The site is still allied to the automotive trade.

The youthful Harry Clayton rides a bicycle, probably on Bridge Avenue, in 1897. He was a longtime partner in the Broad Street men's clothing store, Clayton and Magee, retiring in 1952. Clayton's service record is lengthy, including positions on the Red Bank council, chairmanship of the police committee, its boards of health and education, and the West Side Hose Company. He was survived by his second wife, the former Florence Voorhees.

Harry Clayton built this Four Square, shingle-clad house at 364 Shrewsbury Avenue *c.* 1912; it is shown here *c.* 1930. The house looks similar today, with additions made for its current occupancy by Child's Funeral Home.

Harry Clayton in a rowboat *c.* 1915 became the local photographer's equivalent of *Max Schmitt in a Single Scull*. Clayton had more adventurous maritime interests, evidenced by his membership in the Monmouth Boat Club and honorary status in the North Shrewsbury Ice Boat and Yacht Club.

Harry Clayton married Jennie McQueen in 1907, the year of this picture near their home on the Navesink River that reminds us that the stem west of the bridges can provide pleasant surroundings for small craft boating. Jennie died in 1948.

Jennie Clayton, Ruth Breuer's mother, appears in her millinery splendor around 1920. The collar is not bad, either.

These watermelon eaters of *c.* 1915 seem to have their enjoyment constrained by a need to appear feminine with a sometimes messy refreshment. Bertha Hubbard is in front, and appears to have just bitten a pit. Standing are Cordelia Davis and Josephine McQueen, both forcing smiles. Daisy Davis is caught in the act.

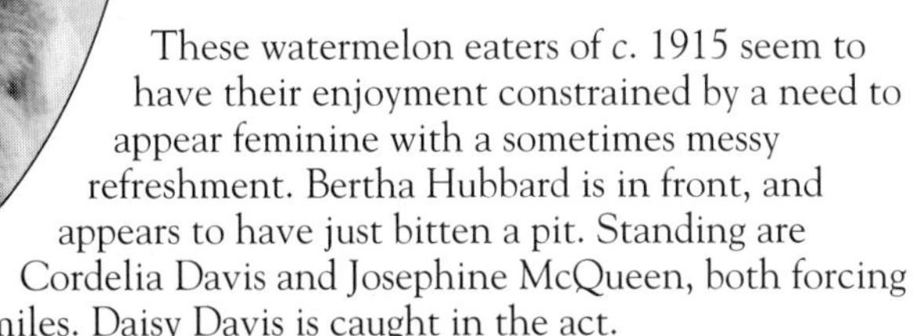

Ruth J. Breuer, daughter of Harry and Jennie Clayton, strikes an attractive pose with her cocker spaniel "Christie" in 1942.

Perhaps the Clayton family ate the rabbits, but the pheasant was stuffed, as Ruth Breuer recalls it being around long after this c. 1924 photograph. Harry Clayton is on the left with his brother Bill.

The Shrewsbury Avenue/Newman Springs Road intersection had the start of its contemporary look with gas stations on its two eastern corners *c.* 1940. The site of the expanded Pleasant Inn, the former Mecca Inn, on the northwest corner is now a gas station, too. The busy stem of Shrewsbury Avenue south of Newman Springs Road was undeveloped then. (The Dorn's Collection.)

River Street at Shrewsbury Avenue in 1955 characterized the pleasant residential streets of the West Side.

Six

People, Places, and Events

An unidentified man stands beside his seemingly unmountable bicycle *c.* 1890, likely on the Fisher estate near the river. (From a glass plate owned and printed by Karen L. Schnitzspahn.)

Local businessmen formed a Roosevelt League of Red Bank to support the "Bull Moose" campaign of the former president. They sponsored a "Stand With Him" rally at the borough hall on Thursday, May 23, 1912, preparatory to Theodore Roosevelt's visit to the Red Bank railroad station on Saturday morning, the 25th. Joseph Dickopf took the photograph.

President Franklin D. Roosevelt visited Red Bank on August 24, 1939, after a reported fishing trip in the North Atlantic. He arrived in local waters on the cruiser *Tuscaloosa* and was transferred to the destroyer *Lang*, which anchored at Fort Hancock in Sandy Hook. He followed the same auto route that was traveled by England's king and queen that June (Volume I, p. 93). After conversing at Red Bank with two clergymen, the president traveled north by train en route to Washington.

The letters of Albert C. Harrison of Company C, 14th Regiment of New Jersey Volunteers, from Camp Hooker were preserved, and many were published in Bernard A. Olsen's *Upon the Tented Field*. Perhaps Harrison did not expect to remain there long, as he wrote on October 18, 1862, "We have enough troops in the field to sweep the whole rebellion out of existence, and the movement will soon be made." Following that November's election, his tone differed. On November 9 he wrote, "I hear the Democrats have carried the day throughout the state, so I expect the war will soon be brought to a close, if that is the case."

Albert C. Harrison, the grandson of Revolutionary War soldier Anthony Dennis, was born c. 1844 around Rumson at the Dennis farm. He fought throughout the Civil War, married Eliza Chadwick after it, and participated in varied business activities. Harrison served thirty-one years as municipal clerk, first for the Township of Shrewsbury and then for Red Bank following the town's separation. He is seen in his borough office in March 1911. He died in 1925. Both Harrison photographs were preserved and lent by his granddaughter, Alma Harrison.

The amateur photographer could freeze a moment in time in a unique manner and in places missed by the professionals. Was a visitor with a camera waiting for a train in the 1890s along with the carriages? He captured a view of the north side of Monmouth Street, the only Red Bank picture in a Middletown album owned by Alice Robinson.

The busy state of an active and fully-occupied Broad Street created the practical effect of Broad wrapping around to embrace some of its side streets, as depicted in this *c.* 1950 view of Linden Place. The popular Churchin's Barber Shop was demolished when the former Strand Theatre was expanded as an office *c.* 1992. Bernard Kellenyi designed the front of the Red Bank Book Store, which reminds one of a time when nearly all business towns had bookstores. Note that Linden Place's one-way traffic was opposite today's west-to-east flow.

British and American flags decorated the route of King George VI and Queen Elizabeth during their June 10, 1939, visit to Red Bank. The royals traveled from the railroad station along Monmouth Street, seen here looking west, to Tower Hill and then along Rumson Road to their Sandy Hook destination (Volume I, p. 93). The building at top right, perhaps best known for its former occupant Mount-English Ford, is at Monmouth's northwest corner with Maple Avenue. Von Kattengill's, the mansard-roofed building on the southeast corner, closed in 1995 after over nine decades of automobile sales. (*Monmouth Pictorial*, Summer 1939.)

In 1927, S.S. Thompson & Company, a substantial Monmouth County contractor, built a 22-by-90 feet, five-story, hollow tile and concrete headquarters building on the north side of Monmouth Street on the east side of the New Jersey Southern tracks. The ground floor served as a showroom for their Hupmobile dealership. It is difficult today to contemplate a rail crossing on Monmouth. Thompson became bankrupt in the early 1930s. This view is *c.* 1940 when the *Red Bank Standard* was a principal tenant. (The Dorn's Collection.)

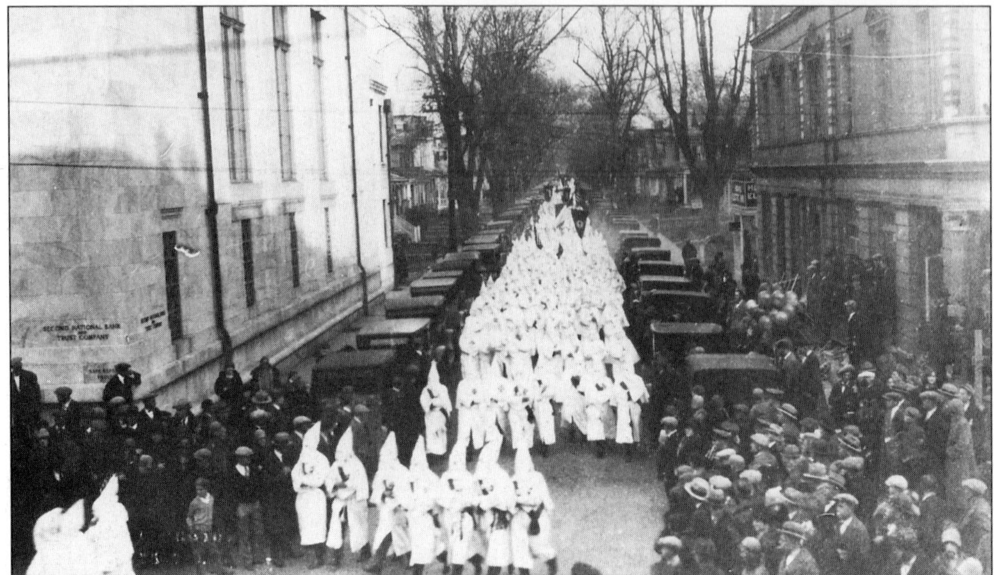

The Ku Klux Klan was recognized by those who did not have their heads buried in the sand as a hate group in the 1920s, the group's heyday on the shore. The Red Bank group received a parade permit in 1923 by virtue of the borough council's overruling the denial by Mayor William H.R. White. They are assembling on Wallace Street at Broad, in an event that was turned into a town-wide Armistice Day celebration in order to dwarf the Klan's participation. (The Dorn's Collection.)

Four musical members of a retirees club called the Old Guard were recalled by Marian Cogan as a long-enduring ensemble who enthralled audiences with their enthusiasm as well as their musicianship. They played at weekly meetings as well as events for outside groups, donning white jackets for those affairs. Cogan remembers Bill Hackett as the violinist, Harry Roede playing the wash tub, Charles De Gavre at the piano, and her father William F. Cogan playing the sax in this *c.* 1960 photograph.

A local fife and drum corps was photographed in August 1893, their spiffy uniforms conveying confidence in their readiness for martial music.

The Union Hose Company No. 1 was organized as the West Red Bank Hose Company in 1890, choosing the present name when incorporating in 1897. Their Shrewsbury Avenue firehouse was built in 1907. The members are posed *c.* 1912 in front of their combination chemical and hose apparatus purchased in 1910.

Windsor Canadian became a major sponsor of the National Sweepstakes Regatta in 1974. Festivities that year included a beauty contest to select the National Regatta Queen and Miss Windsor Canadian. The contestants are lined up on Wharf Avenue that June with Vicki Livingston at left; she was named Miss Windsor Canadian.

Albert L. Ivins, famed marksman, was virtually unbeatable locally in trap shooting competitions. He is seen at the crowning achievement of his career, winning the Grand American Handicap in Cleveland, Ohio, on August 27, 1920, his fifty-second birthday. Missing his sixth clay bird, he hit the next ninety-four, and his score defeated over 750 of the nation's best shooters. He was born in Little Silver, lived at 108 South Street, had a real estate and insurance business in Red Bank, lived to a ripe old age (becoming fondly known as "Uncle Al"), and died in 1954.

Dorothy and George Blair performed in *The Nutcracker* with the Dorothy Toland Dance Studio at the then Carlton Theatre on October 28, 1950. Dorothy, a homecoming queen at Wayne State University who had worked as a part-time dance instructor, was later a board member of the Monmouth Civic Ballet and Monmouth Arts Council. She is better known for her political career, serving the Borough of Shrewsbury twelve years as mayor after her name became Manson through remarriage.

Don Budge, then America's outstanding tennis player, visited Red Bank on June 4, 1940, for a tennis clinic at the municipal courts. After speaking on the game's fundamentals, Budge played an exhibition set with Howard Potter, coach of the high school team. He then paired with Davey Wood, former tennis star at Red Bank High School, playing doubles with Potter and Nelson Ross. Two years earlier, Budge became the first man to win the Grand Slam; he won the American, Australian, English, and French championships in a single year. (*Monmouth Pictorial*, Summer 1940.)

The interior of Dorn's Photo Shop in the 1950s is packed to fulfill the store's reputation as "The Complete Photo Shop." Dan Dorn Sr. and Charlie Ostrander are waiting on customers. Today there may be little demand for the Graflex, but some older equipment may make return appearances in the "used" department, such as those classic twin lens reflexes. The elder Dan may still be seen around the shop, although son Dan Jr. is now the proprietor. Charlie has left, but his brother Eddie, who runs the blueprint and color laser operation, is nearing a half-century of service at Dorn's. (The Dorn's Collection.)

Although some Broad side streets may be virtual extensions of the main business thoroughfare, attention-grabbing signage helps distinguish them. Dorn's Photo Shop has been at 15 Wallace Street since 1946. The huge camera has been used since 1942, earlier hanging at a store on the other side of Wallace. A one-story brick addition was completed in March 1979, with the sign being re-hung over the new section. The affable Dan Dorn Jr. and the irresistible Kathy Dorn Severini make sure it is in focus.

Richard Kirby is the third
generation to run the family leather
goods and harness shop founded by
his grandfather in 1879. It is the sole
survivor of five old, similar
establishments. Dick is seen *c.* 1960s
talking to a passer-by at the east side
of the Wharf Avenue store. He still
talks about the business, now at the
rear of 21 Linden Place.

Dick Kirby is making a point on
leather work to his colleague at his
Wharf Avenue shop *c.* 1960s. The
nature of the business has changed,
with the shop doing repairs on a
variety of leather goods and
manufacturing small items.

The armory at Chestnut and West Streets was completed in 1914 for Troop B of the Red Bank Cavalry. The building, of Norman architectural influence, was designed by the state architect with changes made by Joseph Swannell, captain and quartermaster sergeant of the troop and a Red Bank architect. The main part of the first floor, a riding hall 100-by 144-feet suitable for drills on horseback, is now used for a variety of purposes, including exhibitions. (The Dorn's Collection.)

A Moderne classic would stand at 31 Oakland Street had this building been built to the design Alexander Kellenyi made for Henry Zobel. Believed to have been built for another owner as offices, the stucco and brick building is now occupied as apartments. Kellenyi was a Red Bank architect, born in Budapest, with commissions in several area towns. One is the Mount-English service station in Volume I on p. 118, a building with design similarities to this one. Alexander is the father and professional inspiration of Bernard Kellenyi, whose work is illustrated herein.

110

Howland B. Jones admired Bernard Kellenyi's showroom for Rassas and wanted a similar one at 100 Newman Springs Road. This example was designed with a drive-in service area, a relatively new feature in the early 1950s. Kellenyi recalls Jones's meticulous approach to storage, following the maxim, "a place for everything and everything in its place," a piece of wisdom the author would love to embrace someday. The building still stands, occupied by another dealer.

Luigi's restaurant relocated in the 1950s from a spot near the railroad station to Newman Springs Road, a heavily-trafficked automobile route. Bernard Kellenyi designed the pylon, a popular feature in that period, to catch the motorist's eye. A larger building is on the site now.

This view looks west on Monmouth Street from Broad in the early 1950s. The store in the Swift Building, at right, had not yet been built outside the building line. The third of the three-story structures is the telephone building, remodeled as the borough hall. Part of the Rexall drugstore, built on the site of the former First Methodist Church (p. 30), is visible at left. (The Dorn's Collection.)

The Sears store that occupied the north side of White Street west of English Plaza is seen in the 1950s. Can Beetle buffs spot any year-distinguishing characteristics on this example? The store closed c. 1960s to move to the highway in Middletown. (The Dorn's Collection.)

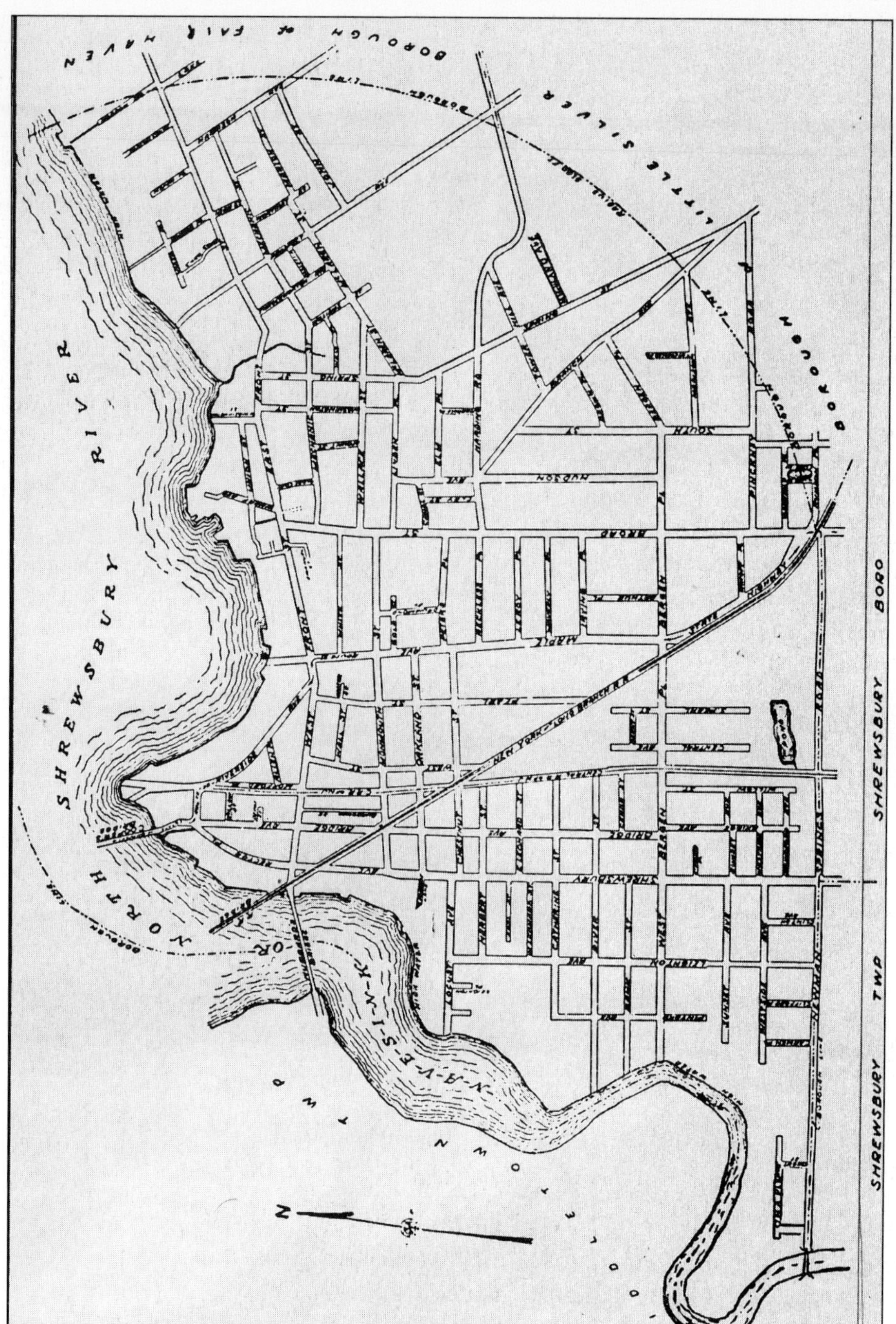

This map from the early 1940s, when held sideways, provides a guide for the aerial photograph on pp. 62 and 63. Note that Bergen Place is the borough's longest street. The New York and Long Branch tracks bisect the town, with few crossings south of Chestnut Street. The eastern border is an arc, a line that was as confusing as it is fascinating. It bisected individual properties, raising the expected complications. The separations with Fair Haven and Little Silver were adjusted through negotiated agreements, resulting in the present saw-toothed border.

The All American Soap Box Derby involved a series of local competitions sponsored by newspapers and Chevrolet dealers. Winners competed in Akron, Ohio, for the national championship. Boys built their non-powered vehicles following derby guidelines, mounting them on standard wheels. The design was crucial in aiding rapid descent on a downhill course. They raced in three-car heats to earn a place in the finals. How did Dorn's finish in 1940? First in photographs! (The Dorn's Collection.)

Richard "Dick" Doughty, a fifteen-year-old Fair Haven resident, won the 1941 soap box derby, the last pre-World War II race in what was then Red Bank's most estimable youth event. Finishing second the year before, Dick made minor modifications to his car for this race, and the design enhancements boosted his performance. He competed that year in Akron, Ohio, with the other regional winners, finishing first in the hearts of Red Bankers, if not in the national competition.

The west side of Hudson Avenue at the point south of Harding Road is shown here on December 27, 1947, following one of the great snowfalls of the century. Three houses on the avenue have since been demolished for the construction of the rear entrance to the Broad Street post office.

Oakland Street looking east at the juncture of the New York and Long Branch and New Jersey Southern tracks is seen here c. 1900. The buildings closest to the tracks are gone, including the Monmouth Ice Company; most were replaced by parking lots. The house behind the ice company stands at No. 80, as does the Oakland Street School (Volume I, p. 102), which has been remodeled as a restaurant without its cupola. The tower of the First Baptist Church of Red Bank is in the distance on the right. (Collection of Glenn Vogel.)

Lewis O. Summersett, with an unidentified assistant, is in the office of *The Mail and Express*, a newspaper he founded in his home in 1900 for a primarily African-American readership. The office was at 37 West Front Street when this picture appeared in Norton's 1904 directory of Red Bank and surrounding towns. No copy of the paper is known to exist.

Frank B. Updyke's Live and Let Live harness shop was established the year prior to this illustration in the July 1911 *American Suburbs*. Updyke was located at 6 Mechanic Street and claimed his $20 Blue Ribbon harnesses and $32 farm harnesses were unexcelled in durability and beauty of finish. The two figures, who almost seem to be differently attired clones, were not identified, although no doubt at least one is Frank. The store is one in a row remodeled into offices.

Columbia Poultry Farm

Frank H. Hodges, Proprietor.
RED BANK, N. J.

White Leghorns   Buff Leghorns
Brown Leghorns   Buff Cochins
Buff & B. Rocks   W. P Rocks
W. C. B. Polish   Black Minorcas
S. S. Hamburgs   Light Brahmas
B. B. R. Games   Black Orpingtons
R. I. Reds   White, Buff and
Partridge Wyandottes, etc.
All varieties of Bantams, Fancy Pigeons, Belgian Hares, Cavies, Pointers and Bull Terriers.

Stock for sale at all times and eggs for setting constantly on hand.

Reference: First National Bank of Red Bank

TELEPHONE, 6-M

Hodges, whose delivery wagon is in Volume I on p. 125, raised a variety of chicken species per this ad from Norton's 1904 directory of Red Bank and surrounding towns. Mabel, the former Mrs. Hodges, had been in charge of the place with five to six hundred chickens. She was born in England, the daughter of a man who lost his prosperity through Wall Street speculation and an experienced horsewoman who regularly drove her husband to the Red Bank station for his rail commute to New York. Mabel died in May 1900 from injuries suffered in a horse runaway accident.

The triangle formed by Branch Avenue, barely shown at left in this *c.* 1960s photograph, and Harding Road was the site of Red Bank's early post-elementary school educational facilities. The 1901 high school, at left and in Volume I on p. 105, was demolished in 1977 following the opening of Red Bank Regional High School in Little Silver. The 1901 school had been converted to a junior high school after the structure in the center was built in 1917-19 as a new high school. The rear of that building represents its 1959 addition. The building at right is the gymnasium addition of a complex that is now the Red Bank Middle School .

Grace Holmes of Shrewsbury, at the top in the center, was a member of the Red Bank High School Class of 1897. Her copy of the class picture was given to the Monmouth County Historical Association, so she is the only one identified. The most distinguished graduate may have been Thomas Irving Brown, who became publisher of the *Register*. The author suspects he is in the middle of the second row, but the identification is not positive.

This Mechanic Street School group posed around 1885.

The 1949 first grade of the Mechanic Street School is shown here. The first boy in line is Joseph Patalano, son of the lenders Daniel and Mary Patalano. If the author had grown up on Red Bank's east side, this would have been his class.

The Red Bank High School baseball team is shown here *c.* 1915. Professor Elmer Woods, at left, was the athletic instructor.

Evelyn Leavens, right, struck an imperious pose, even at age ten. If she appeared to be the princess of the neighborhood, be mindful it was a small realm, as Evelyn was not allowed to cross River Road to visit the store on p. 124. At left is Elizabeth "Betsy" Hall, later Albert, diplomatically called Evelyn "our leader." Their companion, Jean Tilton, died as a youth, while Evelyn and Betsy remain friends. The photograph, dated August 24, 1934, was taken by Samuel Tilton.

An unprotected intersection at Shrewsbury Avenue's juncture with West Front Street and Rector Place seems dangerous beyond imagination today. A fence on the east and a mound on the west impair already limited visibility *c.* 1940s. One wonders how many accidents were needed to secure a traffic control. The street has been widened, with turning lanes recently placed on both sides. (The Dorn's Collection.)

Many Red Bank churches can trace their roots to the Forum, a meeting hall built c. 1825 by public subscription and used for various gatherings in addition to services by many denominations. It was built near the Globe Hotel, near today's Globe Court, and was moved nearby to Mechanic Street at an unspecified time. It was moved again in 1894 to a distant spot on an extension of Mechanic Street when a stable/carriage house was built on Mechanic behind the Globe. The Forum, also used as a school, was destroyed by fire.

The interior of the St. Nicholas Russian Eastern Orthodox church in the 1970s shows its Russian theme decorations. The edifice at 15 Pearl Street was built in 1910 as the Pilgrim Baptist Church (Volume I, p. 108), and that congregation moved to Shrewsbury Avenue in 1955.

Artist Karen Swenson Todd's magnum opus, a five-panel painting of acrylic on wood simply labeled *The Mural*, is a work of broad scope embracing three themes laid out horizontally. At the top, the life of Jesus is represented through reproduction of stained glass windows in the First Baptist Church of Red Bank's sanctuary at the southwest corner of Maple Avenue and Oakland Street. The history of the church is outlined along a center band, while the bottom of the mural portrays the life of the spirit. The church commissioned the mural in 1993 to celebrate the 150th anniversary of the gathering of the congregation and the 100th anniversary of the present building. The mural was conceived, designed, and executed by the artist, with the work done in secret to avoid the comments of on-lookers. Ms. Todd made preliminary sketches, but the work evolved with its progress, aided by her devotion as a parishioner. The history in the center includes the Forum at left, an early non-denominational meeting site (p. 121). The Baptist faith practices total immersion baptism, done in the early years in the river, also represented on the left with scenes of Henry Hudson's ship and one of the region's best known

landmarks, the Twin Lights in Highlands. An earlier edifice on Front Street and the present church (both Volume I, p. 62), with a residence (now The Annex) in between, follow. At the right are the parsonage at 22 Chestnut Street and the Little Silver home for an assistant pastor. A baby dedication ceremony is depicted at bottom right; the ritual represented here is performed in lieu of baptism in sects where the latter is reserved until a profession of faith can be made. A baptism in the present baptistery is pictured. A reproduction of the Sunday school mural, showing children eager to listen to Jesus, was included as a reminder of how important the children are to the church. Symbolism is throughout, including figures in silhouette, symbolic of the present and future members of the church. The mural's border simulates stained glass through a technique the artist developed using eight layers of paint sealed with acrylic gloss medium and varnish. The author offers his thanks to the Reverend Dr. Edward Vander Hey, whose comment reflected the depth and scope of the work, "Every time I look at it, I see something new." (Photograph by David Todd.)

William Cullington's Italianate house at 27 South Street, built *c.* 1870s, remains standing with few changes, notably an extension of the rear first-floor wing. The house at left, no. 25, now has an exterior chimney. Cullington was a tobacco merchant; his Front Street store is shown on the top of p. 52.

Evelyn Leavens drew the former store at 230 Mechanic Street opposite Count Basie's family home. This is a replica of a print given to him. The place has a nostalgia value for Evelyn who still remembers its wide display of penny candy and her frustration over not being permitted to cross River Road to visit it. Fortunately, a friend was able to do her shopping, literally brown-bagging her take from candy heaven. Can you imagine the princess of Alston Court needing to use a runner?

The Reverend William Durnell of Trinity Episcopal Church built this Gothic Revival cottage at 31 Rector Place in 1867. No old picture is known to exist; this contemporary one was included by popular request. Durnell had extensive real estate investments. The building is vacant, a fine subject for restoration.

Fire and neglect have left one of Red Bank's finest Italianate houses in boarded-up condition at 41 Rector Place. It was built *c.* 1870s, with the ells on the sides added later. This fire scene dates from February 4, 1977, when the building was the Richardson Group Home for emotionally disturbed children. Fire damage was repaired before its current decline.

The Prospect Boarding House, long owned by the Borden family and the principal guest house of eastern Red Bank, was so named for the fine view it offered of its surrounding area. Located on Prospect Avenue atop Borden Hill, now Tower Hill, the building and about sixteen acres were sold to Monroe Eisner in 1919. Eisner demolished the old place to build the house pictured below. A *c.* 1860s view of the hill can be seen in a painting by an unidentified artist from the Gordon farm, featured in the author's 1994 *Middletown Township*, published by Arcadia.

In 1919 Monroe Eisner built this Tudor Revival house designed by Red Bank architect Fred Truex, shown here in a *c.* 1930 postcard image. It was on the west side of Prospect Avenue, today the site of the Tower Hill condominiums. (Collection of John Rhody.)

A different camera angle in this *c.* 1915 photograph makes the Abram I. Elkus 1906 Colonial Revival house even more attractive than it seems in the image featured in Volume I on p. 114. Little has been revealed about the house's origins, other than the fact that it was started by Henry J. Randall and sold to Elkus in 1906. It is the site of the Presbyterian church's hall, having served as its education building until it was demolished for the present structure *c.* 1960.

The hall of the Abram I. Elkus house, shown here in a *c.* 1915 photograph, reflects a high-design interior. The house was one of the finest Colonial Revivals ever built in Red Bank.

Robert R. Campbell, a member of the Class of 1944, is carrying the flag at a 1942 Red Bank High School football game. He entered the army in August 1943 under an early-release program and left for North Africa around February 1944. That May, as his classmates were preparing for graduation, Campbell made the supreme sacrifice around Anzio, Italy. His memory is commemorated by the Robert Rue Campbell Award, which is presented by Shrewsbury Borough School seniors to a class member who best exemplifies the twelve personal qualities used as the award's criteria.

The Walter L. Main Three Big Ring Circus advertised its August 6, 1927 coming to Red Bank, touting a "show of supremely stupendous surprises" and a "peerless program of pre-eminent performers," messages clearly generated by an annoyingly alliterative adwriter. The locale of this view is not clear. The circus began with a 1-mile parade at 11:00 am, likely between the railroad station and Highway 35, as they proceeded to the circus grounds at Crescent Parkway and Iroquois Street in Middletown. An enlarged cover of this book would look great on the wagon!